48/04

cc∅

J B
MHS

MAY 2 0 1992

A ROOKIE BIOGRAPHY

LOUIS PASTEUR

Enemy of Disease

By Carol Greene

CHILDRENS PRESS ®
CHICAGO

This book is for Peg Cooper.

Louis Pasteur (1822-1895)

Library of Congress Cataloging-in-Publication Data

Greene, Carol.
    Louis Pasteur : enemy of disease / by Carol Greene.
        p.   cm. — (A Rookie biography)
    Summary: A simple biography of the French scientist who proved the
existence of germs and their connection with disease.
    ISBN 0-516-04216-5
    1. Pasteur, Louis, 1822-1895—Juvenile literature. 2. Scientists—France—
Biography—Juvenile literature. 3. Microbiologists—France—Biography—
Juvenile literature. [1. Pasteur, Louis, 1822-1895. 2. Scientists.
3. Microbiologists.] I. Title. II. Series: Greene, Carol. Rookie biography.
Q143.P2G74   1990
540′.92—dc20
[B]
[92]   90-2197
                                                                      CIP
                                                                       AC

Louis Pasteur
was a real person.
He was born in 1822.
He died in 1895.
Pasteur was a scientist.
His work has saved
millions of lives.
This is his story.

TABLE OF CONTENTS

Louis Pasteur was born in Dôle, France. The Pasteur family moved to Arbois when Louis was a young boy.

Chapter 1

The Wolf

"Watch out!
It's a mad wolf!
It's biting people!"
That news made people
in Arbois, France,
shake with fear.

Louis Pasteur lived in Arbois.
He was eight years old.
He knew that the bite
of the mad wolf could kill
people and animals.

Then the wolf bit a neighbor.
Louis saw someone put
a hot iron on the bites.
That looked horrible.
But the neighbor lived.
Eight other people died.
The bites from the mad
wolf killed them.

Louis never forgot that wolf.

**A small village
in France**

But he was a busy boy.
He played with his sisters.
He went fishing
with his friends.
He went to school.

Louis Pasteur drew these portraits
of his father and mother.

At school, he worked
slowly and carefully.
Louis wanted everything
he did to be *right*.

He loved to draw
and he was good at it.
He made pictures
of his family
and of other people, too.

Louis thought he might
be an artist someday.
But his high school principal
said he should be a professor.

So Louis studied hard.
When he was 15,
he went to school in Paris.
But he got homesick.
Soon his father came
and took him home again.

This portrait of Pasteur
was made while he was
a student at the
École Normale in the
city of Paris.
The city is shown below
as it looked in 1850.

Louis kept working.
He liked science.
When he was 20,
he went to the École Normale,
a school for teachers in Paris.
This time, he didn't get homesick.

Louis had found
the right place for him.
His mind was full of science.
But sometimes he still thought
about the mad wolf of Arbois.

Louis Pasteur in his laboratory

Chapter 2

Crystals and Beet Juice

At the École Normale, Louis
studied chemistry and physics.
He became interested in crystals
and how they grow.

After three years, he got
a job in a laboratory.
He worked with crystals.
But he studied other things, too.

Louis taught chemistry at the University of Strasbourg.

Then Louis made a big discovery
about how crystals act.
Because of his discovery,
he met important scientists.

One of these scientists
helped Louis get a new job.
He would teach chemistry
at the university at Strasbourg.

The city of Strasbourg, France, about 1870

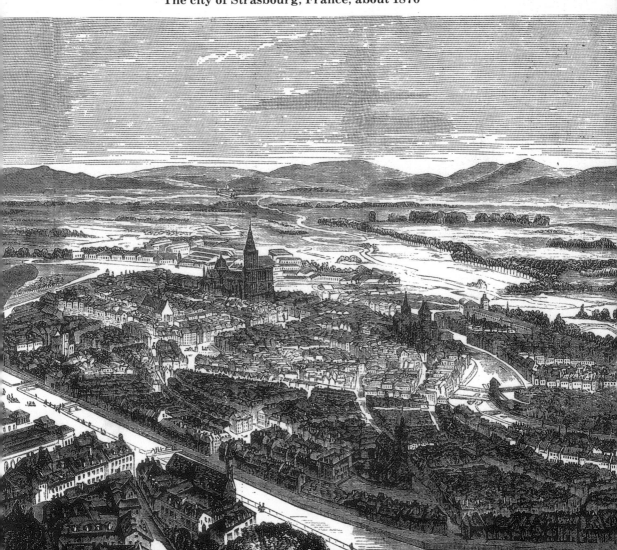

Marie Laurent

There Louis met Marie Laurent.
Louis said he loved her
even more than crystals.
They got married in 1849.

Marie said she wanted
to learn about crystals.
So Louis taught her.
Soon she became his helper.

In 1850, baby Jeanne was born.
In all, the Pasteurs had
four girls and one boy.
Marie said that Louis
was a good father.

Louis kept studying crystals.
His work won prizes.
But then he found something
new to study—beet juice.

Sometimes it turned to alcohol.
Sometimes it just turned sour.
Louis wondered why.

At last he found
tiny, living things
in the beet juice.
They are called microbes,
or germs.

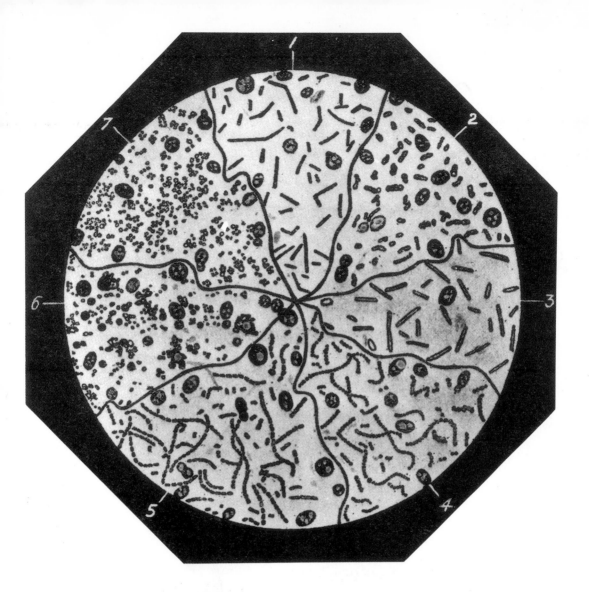

Microbes of different sizes and shapes can be seen under a microscope. The number 2 microbes turn milk sour. The number 1 microbes turn grape juice into wine. Pasteur discovered that different microbes did different things.

Louis learned that different microbes act in different ways. That was why the beet juice acted in different ways. Louis was excited.

Pasteur taught at the
École Normale.
He set up his own small
laboratory (above) and
continued his
experiments.

But he had to stop his experiments
and start a new job.
In 1857, he became head
of science at the École Normale.

It was a fine job.
But Louis had no laboratory.
So he found two little rooms
in an attic at the school
and built his own lab.
Then he got back to his experiments.

Chapter 3

Microbes

In 1859, nine-year-old Jeanne Pasteur
died of typhoid fever.
That hurt Louis.
He worked even harder.
Maybe someday he could
save children from diseases.

At that time, scientists
knew there were microbes.
But they didn't know
where microbes came from.
They thought they just *happened*.

Louis proved that
microbes are in the air.
He also showed that
some air has more microbes
in it than other air.

He thought some microbes
could be dangerous.
They could cause diseases
like Jeanne's typhoid fever.

Pasteur proved that heat
could kill microbes.
Later, people used his idea
to kill the germs, or microbes,
in milk and other foods.
It is called pasteurization.
It has saved many lives.

One hundred years ago, many people got diseases
from drinking milk just as it came from cows.
Today, milk is pasteurized to kill any germs that
may be in the milk.

Louis' work with microbes
helped vinegar makers
make better vinegar.
It helped wine makers
make better wine.

Louis and Marie Pasteur in 1867

Next, Louis studied silkworms.
Silkworms make silk,
and making silk cloth
was a big business in France.
But the silkworms were dying.

At last, Louis found two
diseases in the silkworms.
He found a way to keep
the silkworms healthy, too.

During that time,
Louis' father died.
So did two of his little girls.
Louis felt sad and angry.
Why couldn't he help
the people he loved?

Some people thought
Louis' ideas were wrong.
Louis knew how to fight them.
He worked slowly and carefully
to prove his ideas were right.

Louis Napoleon
was emperor
of France from
1852 to 1871.

Then the emperor of France
said he would build Louis
a fine new lab.
That made Louis work so hard
that he had a stroke.

"I am sorry to die," he said.
"I wanted to do much more
for my country."

But Louis didn't die.
He had fought
for his ideas and won.
Now he fought for his life
and won again.

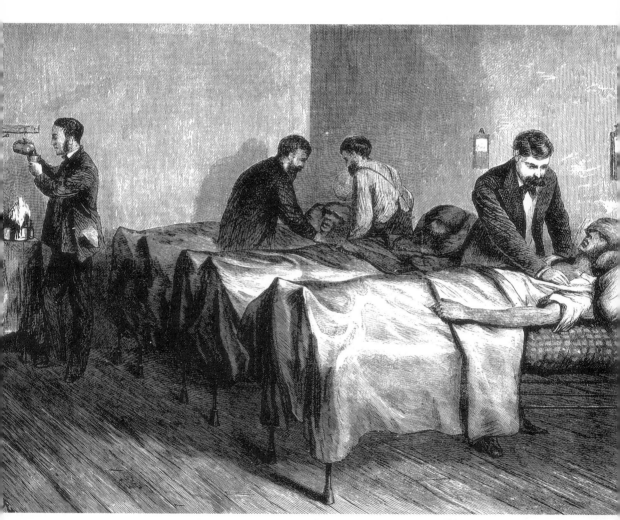

One hundred years ago, hospitals were crowded and dirty places.

Chapter 4

More Microbes

Louis' work helped
his country in many ways.
Now he wanted to work
on diseases that were
killing people.

At that time, hospitals
were dirty, awful places.
Louis said doctors should
boil or heat their tools.
That would kill microbes
and save lives.

He began to study anthrax,
a disease that killed sheep.
He gave shots of weak anthrax
microbes to healthy sheep.
The sheep did not get sick.
Now they were safe.
They didn't get anthrax.
He called this method vaccination.

More and more people
heard about Louis' work.
They gave him prizes and
asked him to make speeches.

Pasteur was given many awards for his work. Here he wears the ribbon of the French Legion of Honor.

Once he went to England.
He heard people in a hall
clapping and cheering.
Louis thought all that noise
was for England's prince.
But it was for *him*.

Many years had gone by.
But Louis had never forgotten
that mad wolf in Arbois.
Now he began to study rabies.

It was hard work.
The rabies microbe was
too small to be seen.
It was dangerous work, too.
Louis could have been bitten.

But in 1884, he learned
how to make the right vaccine.
It kept animals
from getting rabies.
It cured them when
mad animals bit them.

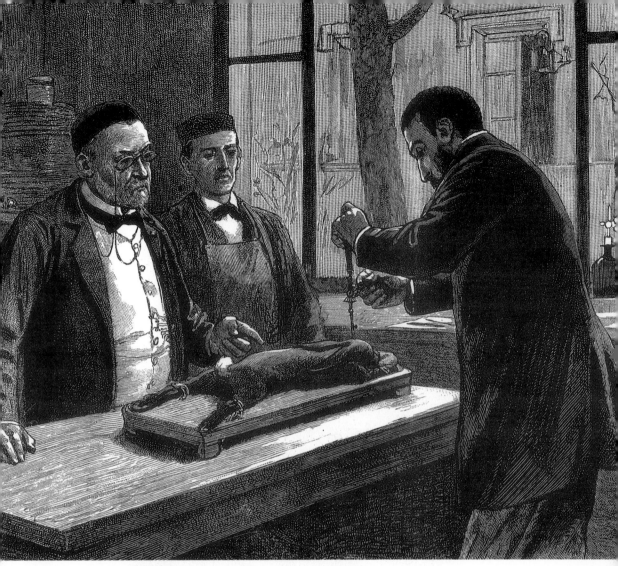

Pasteur experimented with rabbits while developing his animal rabies vaccine.

Louis wanted to try
his rabies vaccine on people.
But he was afraid.
What if it didn't work?

Louis and Marie Pasteur
in 1884 (above).
A statue of Joseph Meister
being bitten by the
mad dog (right).

Chapter 5

The Big Test

On July 6, 1885,
a boy and his mother
came to Louis' lab.
The boy's name was Joseph Meister.
He was nine years old.
A mad dog had bitten him.

Louis counted 14 bites.
They would kill Joseph.
What should Louis do?
Should he give Joseph the vaccine?

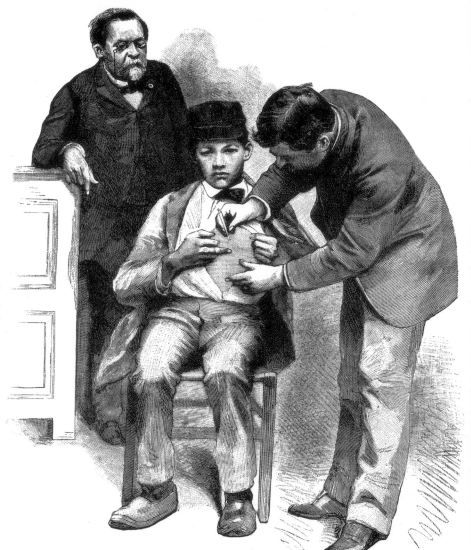

Joseph Meister
receiving a shot
of rabies vaccine

Louis talked to doctors.
"Give him the vaccine," they said.
So Louis did.
He gave Joseph 13 shots.
That was the big test.
And Joseph got well.

Soon after that, the mayor
of a town wrote to Louis.
He said that six children
were watching some sheep
when a mad dog attacked.

Jean, the oldest boy,
fought the dog
so the others could get away.
The dog bit Jean's hands,
but he tied its jaws together.

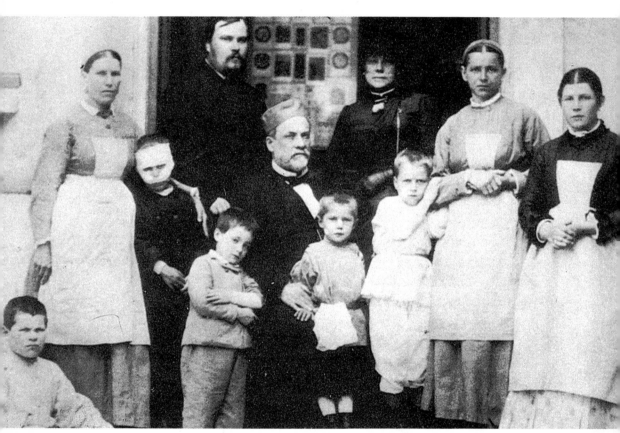

Pasteur with a group of children who had been bitten
by mad dogs and sent to him for inoculation

Louis told the mayor to send
the brave shepherd boy to him.
He gave Jean the rabies shots
and saved his life.

Then many more people
came to Louis for help.
Soon he had treated 350 of them.
All but one lived.

Louis needed new buildings
to help still more people.
When the world heard that,
money came from everywhere.
Rich and poor people sent gifts.
Great rulers and children did, too.

In 1888, the Pasteur Institute
opened its doors in Paris.
Louis was too old and weak
to study diseases anymore.
But he had many helpers.
They went on with his work.

Joseph Meister, the first boy
Louis saved, grew up and came
to work at the Pasteur Institute.

Pasteur at the Pasteur Institute in Paris

He took care of
one of the buildings.
Later, Jean, the shepherd
boy, worked in a lab.

Louis watched his helpers. He talked to children who had been bitten. When they were afraid, he dried their tears and gave them shiny coins.

Pasteur and some of his fellow workers at the Pasteur Institute

Pasteur with two of his grandchildren in 1891

In 1895, Louis died in his home outside Paris. His family and friends were around him. Marie held his hand.

He was buried in a chapel
at the Pasteur Institute.
Soon there were new institutes
all around the world.
Louis Pasteur's work
would never die.

Important Dates

1822   December 27—Born in Dôle, France, to Jean
         Joseph and Jeanne Etiennette Pasteur

1843   Went to École Normale, Paris

1849   Married Marie Laurent

1857   Became manager and director of scientific
         studies at the École Normale

1865   Studied pasteurization

1881   Used vaccine for anthrax

1885   Saved lives of Joseph Meister and Jean
         Baptiste Jupille with rabies treatment

1888   Pasteur Institute founded in Paris

1895   September 28—Died

INDEX

Page numbers in boldface type indicate illustrations.

PHOTO CREDITS

ABOUT THE AUTHOR

Carol Greene has degrees in English Literature and Musicology. She has worked in international exchange programs, as an editor, and as a teacher. She now lives in St. Louis, Missouri, and writes full-time. She has published more than eighty books. Others in the Rookie Biographies series include *Benjamin Franklin, Pocahontas, Martin Luther King, Jr., Christopher Columbus, Abraham Lincoln, Robert E. Lee, Ludwig van Beethoven, Laura Ingalls Wilder, Jackie Robinson, Jacques Cousteau, Daniel Boone, Queen Elizabeth I*, and *Black Elk.*